ALTERNATOR BOOKS™

THE MOON FILES

HISTORY OF MOON EXPLORATION

Beth Adelman

Lerner Publications ◆ Minneapolis

Lerner Publications Company
An imprint of Lerner Publishing Group, Inc.
241 First Avenue North
Minneapolis, MN 55401 USA

For reading levels and more information, look up this title at www.lernerbooks.com.

Main body text set in Aptifer Sans LT Pro.
Typeface provided by Linotype.

Library of Congress Cataloging-in-Publication Data

Names: Adelman, Beth, author.
Title: History of moon exploration / Beth Adelman.
Description: Minneapolis, MN : Lerner Publications, [2025] | Series: Alternator books. The moon files | Includes bibliographical references and index. | Audience: Ages 8–12 | Audience: Grades 4–6 | Summary: "Humans have explored the moon's surface using rovers, probes, and astronauts. Discover the history of moon exploration, what technology was used, and what we have learned as a result"—Provided by publisher.
Identifiers: LCCN 2023049767 (print) | LCCN 2023049768 (ebook) | ISBN 9798765625590 (library binding) | ISBN 9798765629802 (paperback) | ISBN 9798765637845 (epub)
Subjects: LCSH: Space flight to the moon—History—Juvenile literature. | Space race—History—Juvenile literature. | Moon—Exploration—History—Juvenile literature.
Classification: LCC TL799.M6 .A44 2025 (print) | LCC TL799.M6 (ebook) | DDC 629.45/409—dc23/eng/20231107

LC record available at https://lccn.loc.gov/2023049767
LC ebook record available at https://lccn.loc.gov/2023049768

Manufactured in the United States of America
1 – CG – 7/15/24

TABLE OF CONTENTS

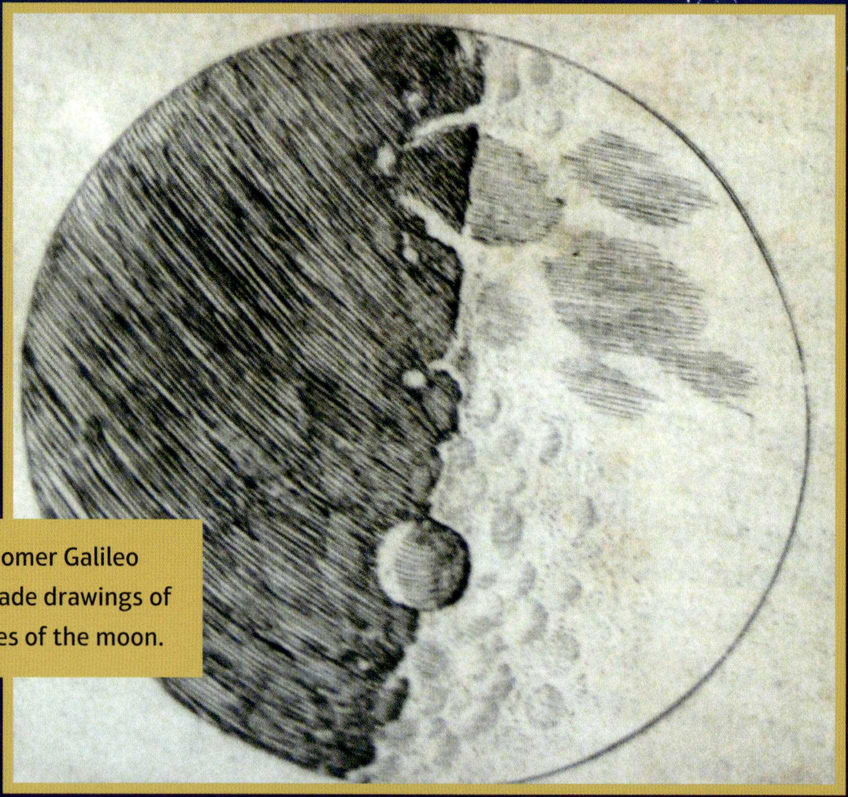

Astronomer Galileo Galileo made drawings of his studies of the moon.

INTRODUCTION

LOOK UP IN THE SKY

On a clear November night in 1609, an Italian astronomer named Galileo Galilei looked up at the moon. He was using a telescope he built himself. Back then, everyone thought the surface of the moon was smooth. But Galileo saw that the patterns of light and shadow on the moon changed over time.

The same thing happens on Earth when shadows cast by a tree or a house are different lengths at different times of the day. Galileo realized there must be mountains on the moon making the shadows.

On a July night 360 years later, the first people walked on the moon. By then dozens of spacecraft had already been there. They sent back information that made it possible for people to land on the moon. The astronauts came home with the first moon rocks humans had ever touched. We were no longer exploring the moon from a distance. Unlike Galileo, we could explore it in person.

There is still much we don't know about our moon. Scientists continue to send probes, landers, and rovers there to learn more. Even better, humans will be returning soon. We're just getting started in our quest to understand the moon.

Apollo 11 astronaut Buzz Aldrin was one of the first humans to walk on the moon.

Sputnik means "traveling companion" in Russian. The satellite was about the size of a beach ball.

CHAPTER 1

THE SPACE RACE

In the 1950s, the United States and the Soviet Union competed to be the most powerful in the world. The Soviet Union was made up of Russia and several other nations. Those nations separated in 1991.

One way to show power was to explore space. Both countries decided to send satellites into space. Satellites orbiting Earth could be used for communications and research.

The Soviet Union got to space first. In October 1957, the Soviet Union launched a satellite called Sputnik 1. It orbited Earth. Just months later, the US Army launched Explorer 1. Its mission was to study radiation around Earth. The space race was on!

The US officially entered the space race with the launch of Explorer 1.

NASA's first space mission sent Pioneer I, an 84 pound (38 kg) probe, into space.

First Glimpses of the Moon

Both countries wanted to send the first space probe to the moon. In October 1958, a new US agency was formed to do that. It was called the National Aeronautics and Space Administration (NASA). That same month, NASA launched its first project, Pioneer 1. The probe was supposed to orbit the moon. But some of its rockets didn't work properly. It was only able to orbit Earth.

The Soviets had a few rocket failures, too. But in January 1959, their probe Luna 1 flew within about 4,000 miles (6,400 km) of the moon. Then it crashed into the sun.

In March, NASA's Pioneer 4 flew past the moon. Like Explorer 1, it carried instruments that studied the moon's radiation levels. Scientists needed to know if astronauts could be harmed by radiation on the moon.

Then in September, the Soviet probe Luna 2 tried to be the first spacecraft to land on the moon. But it crashed. The next month, Luna 3 was the first to take pictures of the dark side of the moon. No human had ever seen it, not even with a telescope.

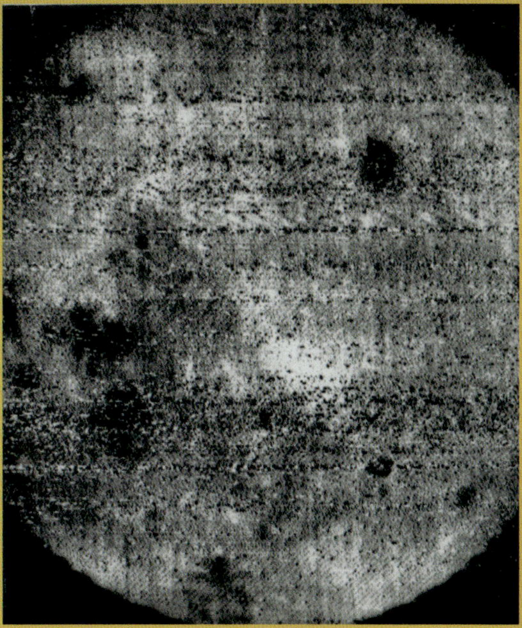

The Soviet Union spacecraft Luna 3 took the first photo of the far side of the moon in October, 1959.

THE FAR SIDE OF THE MOON

The far side of the moon is not dark. It is just hidden from us on Earth. Why doesn't the far side ever face us?

The moon rotates at exactly the same speed that it orbits Earth. It takes 27.3 days for the moon to make one full orbit around Earth. That's why the same side of the moon is always turned toward Earth.

President John F. Kennedy inspired the nation to put humans on the moon.

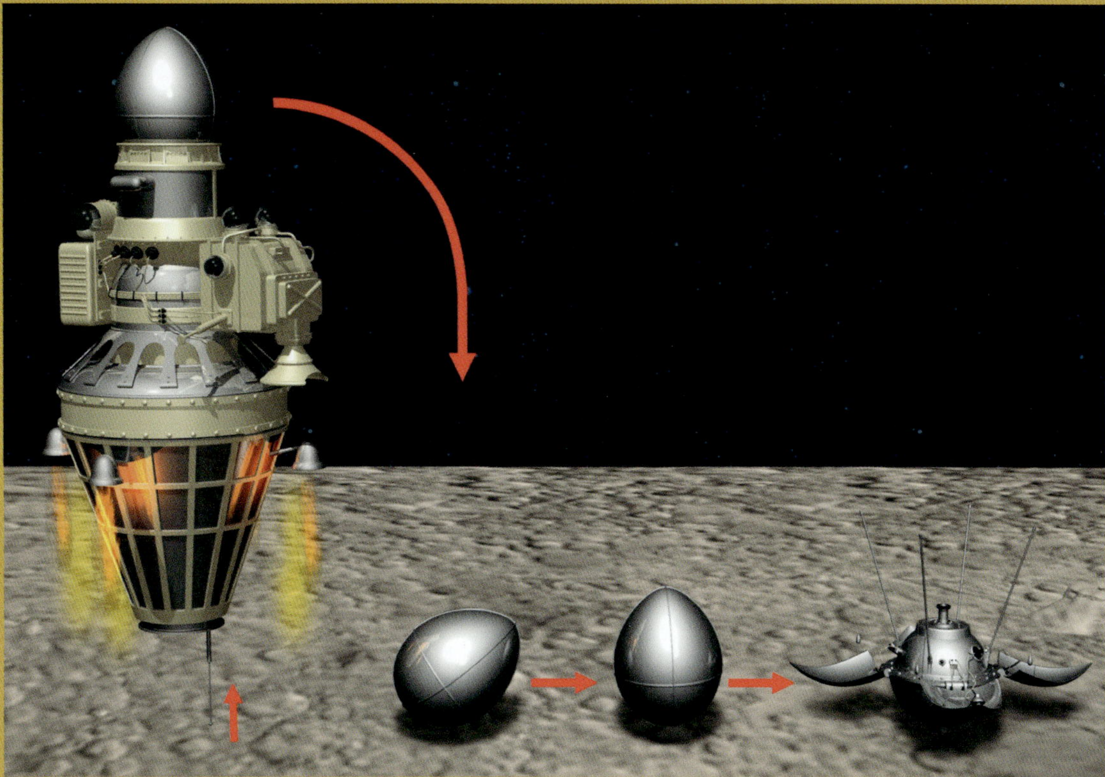

The Luna 9 probe landed on the moon in 1966.

A Promise to Keep

In 1961, President John F. Kennedy made a bold goal. He said the US would send a person to the moon and back before the decade ended. NASA launched nine Ranger probes between 1961 and 1965. They all took detailed pictures of the moon. This helped scientists decide on the safest spot to land.

In 1966, the Soviet probe Luna 9 landed safely on the moon. It didn't crash! In all, there were 24 Luna missions that studied the moon.

NASA's Surveyor missions gathered vital information about the moon.

Probing for Answers

NASA also sent up seven Surveyor probes. These probes carried cameras and small robotic laboratories. They scooped up soil and rock samples and sent the information back to Earth. They tested if it was possible to land on the moon and then take off.

Surveyor probes gathered information scientists needed for the Apollo program. This NASA mission would put humans on the moon. First, there was more to learn about the moon. How hot did it get in the daytime? How cold did it get at night? What kind of spacesuits would protect astronauts on the moon?

Scientists needed to know how solid the moon's surface was before attempting to land a spaceship there.

In 1968, NASA's Apollo 8 put humans into orbit around the moon for the first time. The next year, Apollo 9 and 10 tested the spacecraft that would land on the moon. Each mission got NASA closer to landing on the moon.

Apollo 11 successfully landed on the moon with astronauts aboard. On July 21, 1969, Neil Armstrong stepped out onto the moon. Buzz Aldrin was right behind him. Millions of people around the world watched this historic event on television.

Apollo 11 astronauts had to be quarantined for three weeks after their return to Earth to make sure they didn't bring unknown germs.

Earthrise is a famous image captured by Apollo 8 astronaut Bill Anders.

Apollo 16 was the second space mission to use a lunar vehicle.

CHAPTER 2

OTHERS JOIN THE MISSION

The race to be first to walk on the moon was over. After Apollo 11, NASA landed astronauts on the moon five more times. Even so, they only explored a tiny part of the moon.

Japan launched an orbiting satellite called Hiten in 1990. It tested technologies used to study and land on the moon. The Japanese Aerospace Exploration Agency (JAXA) launched another satellite in 2007. Kaguya carried two much smaller satellites onboard. Together, they created a detailed map of the moon's surface.

Japan's satellite Hiten was named after a flying, music-playing Buddhist angel.

The Far Side of the Moon

The China National Space Administration launched a space program in 2007. Three Chang'e missions mapped certain spots on the moon's surface. These precise maps were used to help plan rover missions and landings.

In 2019 Chang'e 4 made history. It was the first spacecraft to land on the far side of the moon. It sent out a rover called Yutu-2. Chang'e 4 also placed a communications satellite in orbit around the moon. It has to be in exactly the right spot to communicate with both Earth and Yutu-2.

China's rover Yutu-2 explored the far side of the moon.

China's Chang'e-5 returned moon rock and dust samples to Earth in 2020 by dropping off a package in a special spacecraft made to return to Earth.

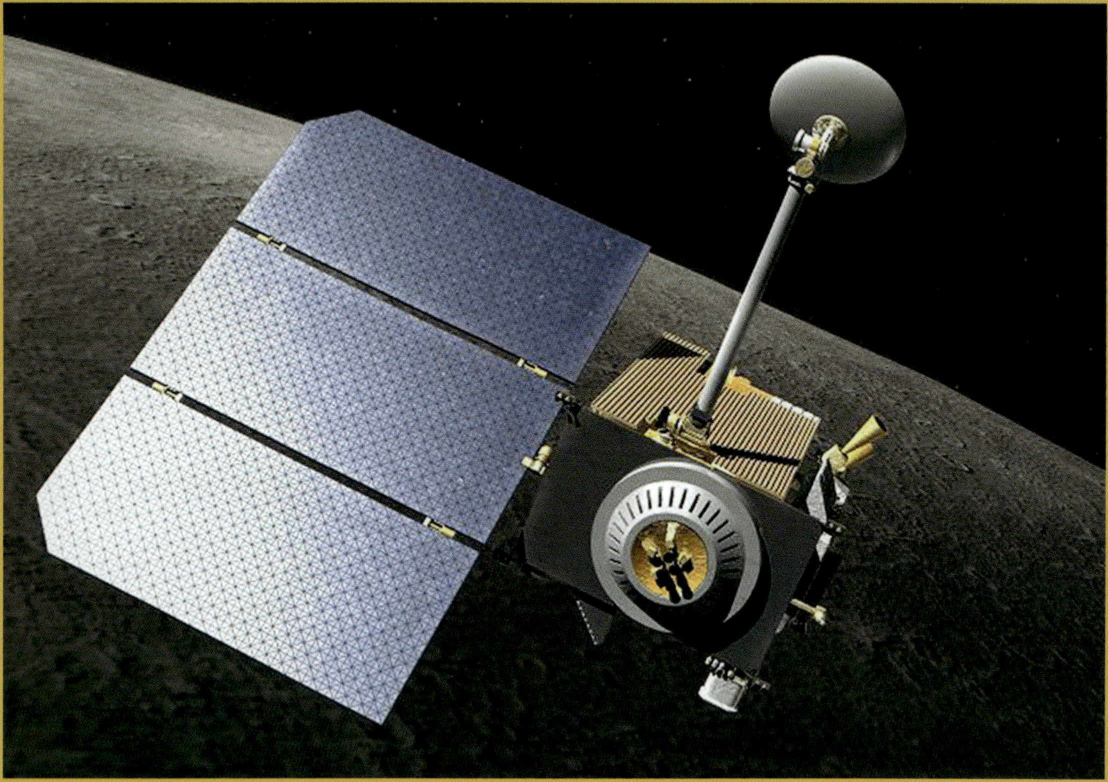

NASA's Lunar Reconnaissance Orbiter detected water ice on the moon's poles.

Icy Discovery

For a long time, scientists thought the moon was completely dry. Astronauts who visited the moon found no signs of water. But in 2008, Chandrayaan-1 changed everything.

The Indian Space Research Organization put Chandrayaan-1 into orbit around the moon. The spacecraft carried scientific instruments from space agencies in several countries. Two of these instruments detected ice from water on the moon!

In August 2023, India made space history with Chandrayaan-3. It was the first spacecraft ever in the moon's south polar region.

WHERE IS THE WATER ON THE MOON?

The moon's north and south poles are two permanently shadowed regions (PSRs). PSRs are where water ice is likely to be.

Scientists estimate that all the PSRs on the poles may hold at least 1.3 trillion pounds (600 million metric tons) of water ice. That is enough water to fill 240,000 Olympic-size swimming pools.

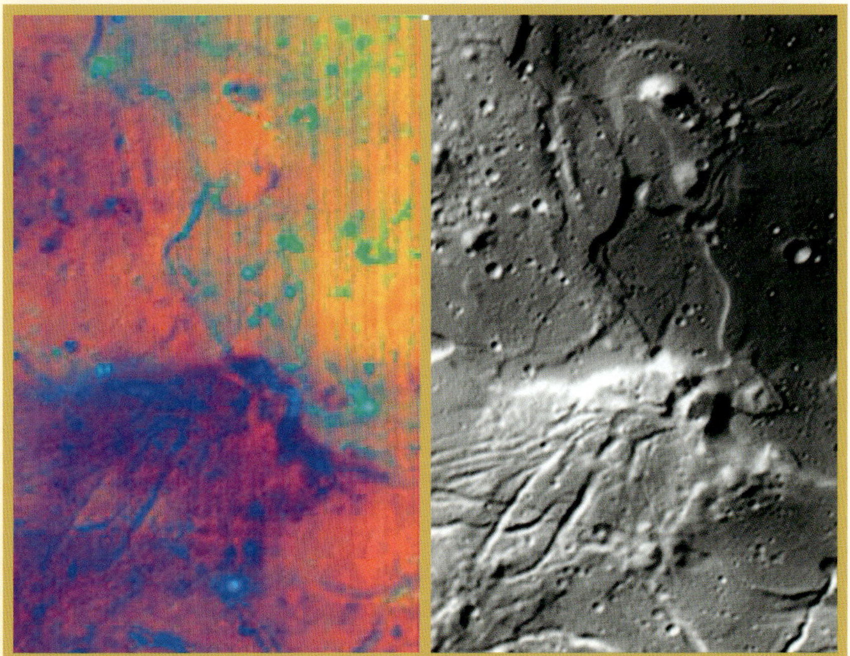

NASA's Moon Mineralogy Mapper, an instrument on the India's Chandrayaan-1 mission, took this image of the moon.

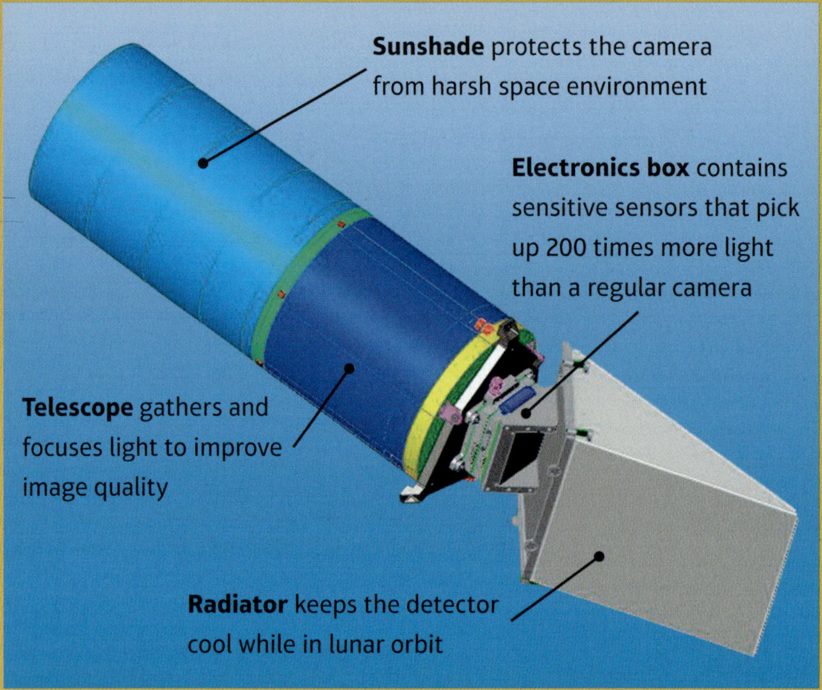

ShadowCam captures images of areas on the moon which never receive direct sunlight called permanently shadowed regions (PSRs).

Space Dance

In 2022, the Korea Aerospace Research Institute launched Danuri. The South Korean lunar orbiter included a NASA instrument called ShadowCam. This device searched for ice in dark craters.

Danuri also tested how a space internet could connect a moon base to Earth. Using a special internet device, Danuri sent photos of Earth back to receivers in South Korea. It also played the music video "Dynamite" by the pop band BTS. This data traveled 74,5645 miles (1.2 million km) from the moon to Earth.

SpaceX launched South Korea's first mission to the moon in 2022.

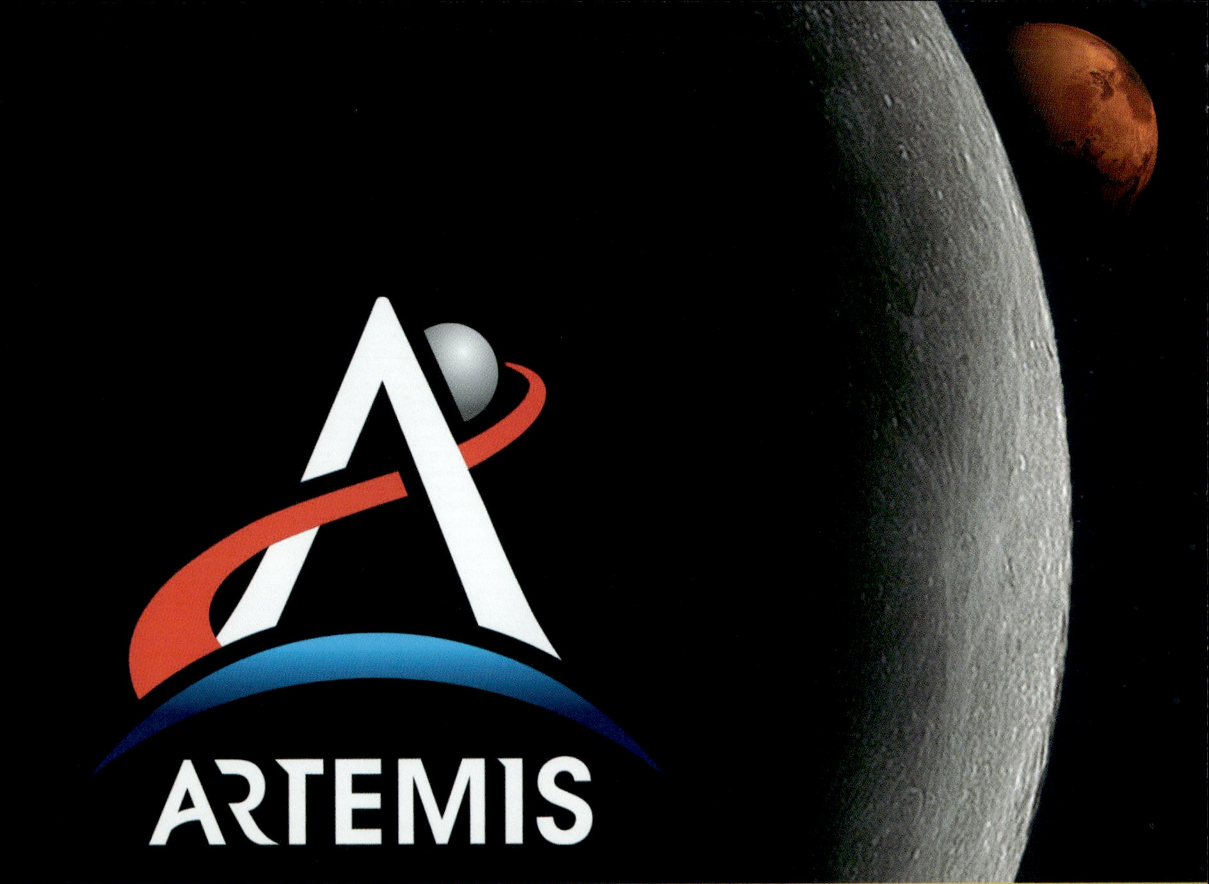

The Artemis program is working on sending humans back to the moon.

CHAPTER 3

WORKING TOGETHER

Humans have not walked on the moon since 1972. But a new program called Artemis plans to send humans back. The plan is to build an orbiting space station. The goal is to one day establish a permanent base on the moon.

Instead of racing against each other, countries are now working together. The US, Canada, Japan, Israel, Australia, and Europe are all part of the Artemis program.

Like the Apollo program, the first Artemis missions are testing the mission's spacecraft. Spacecraft must pass many safety tests before taking humans to the moon. In 2022, Artemis 1 sent the crew capsule Orion to the moon and back. Crash test dummies named Moonikins were on board to make sure everything was safe.

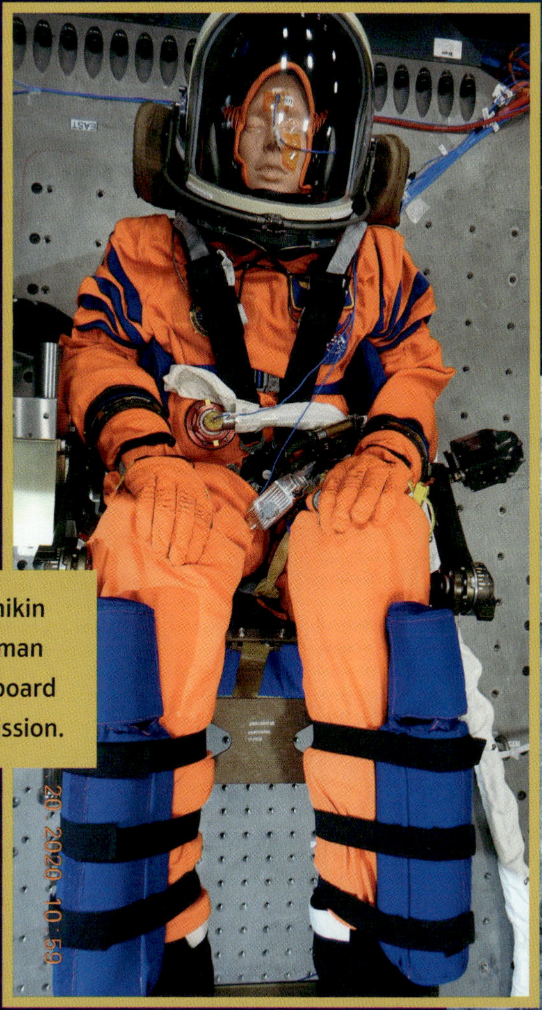

Commander Moonikin Campos, a nonhuman mannequin, was aboard the first Artemis mission.

Artemis 2 astronauts will fly 4,600 miles (7,400 km) farther past the moon than any humans have ever gone in space.

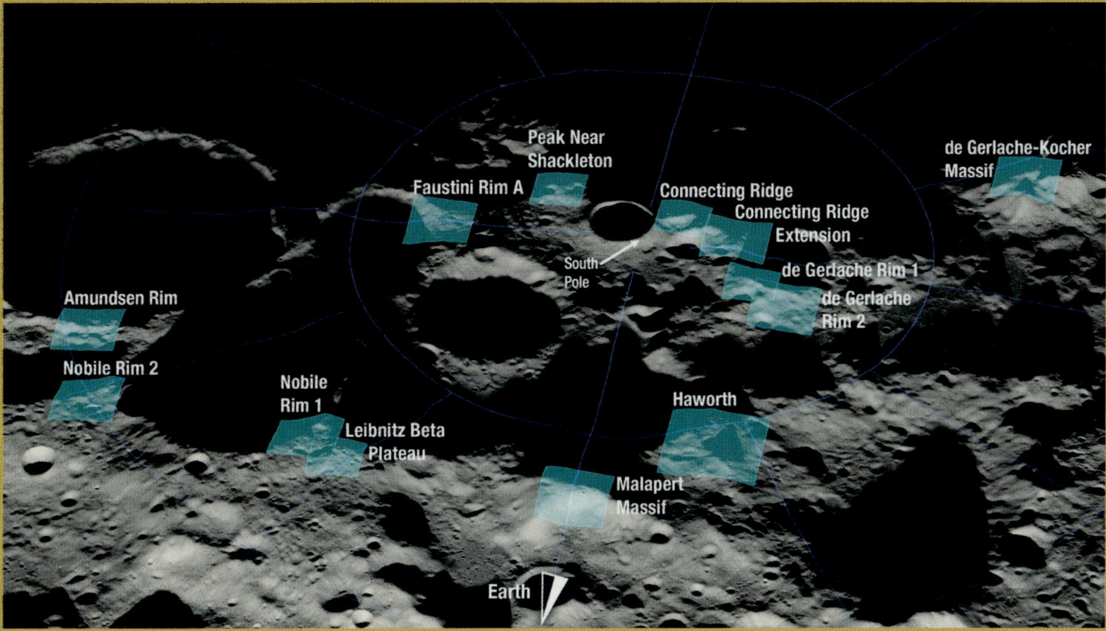

NASA is considering landing Artemis in one of the regions on the moon's south pole.

Back to the Moon

Artemis 2 is planned to launch in 2024 with four astronauts onboard. The astronauts won't get to land on the moon. Instead, they will fly around and far beyond the moon, then return to Earth. The astronauts' job during the flight is to test all the systems on Orion, including the life support and navigation systems.

Finally, in 2025, humans plan to return to the moon with Artemis 3. The plan for Artemis 3 is to land a crew at the moon's south polar region. Two astronauts will land on the surface of the moon and explore for about one week. Two other astronauts will remain aboard the Orion. This mission will include the first woman and person of color to land on the moon.

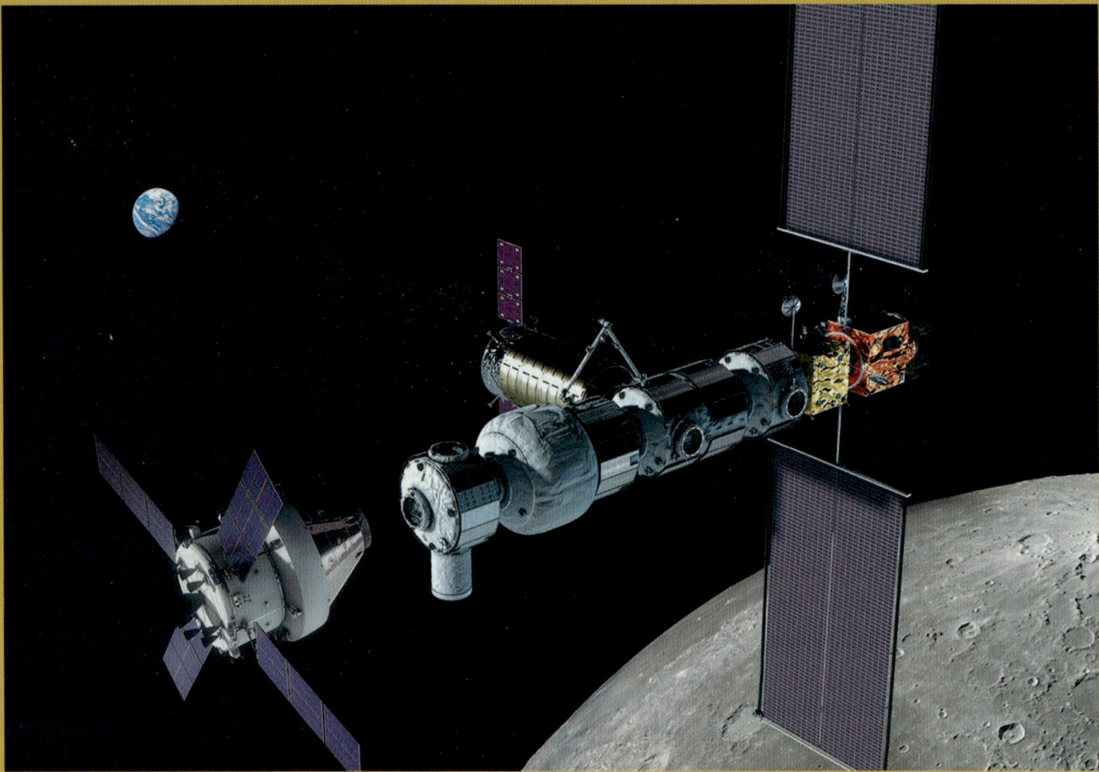

The Lunar Gateway will be an important part of the Artemis 4 mission.

The Moon and Beyond

Artemis 4 is set to land more people on the moon in 2028. The people on Artemis 4 will finish building the Lunar Gateway, the first space station around the moon. Later missions will build a permanent base on the moon. Missions are planned every year after that, all the way through Artemis 11 in 2035.

Living and working on the moon is an exciting idea. But it's just the first step in an even more challenging goal: sending astronauts to Mars. What we learn from exploring the moon will help us figure out how to go even further into space.

After the moon, NASA plans to land humans on Mars.

GLOSSARY

atmosphere: mixtures of gases that surround Earth and some other planets

basalt: a kind of rock formed from rapidly cooling magma

crater: a huge, bowl-shaped dent found on the surface of an object

crust: the outermost layer on a planet or a moon

element: a pure substance, in solid, liquid, or gas form, made of one type of atom; building blocks of everything in the world

erosion: the process of being worn away by wind, water, and other natural forces

gravity: the force by which a planet or other body draws objects toward its center

magma: superhot melted rock below a moon or planet's crust; it becomes lava when it comes to the surface, and once it hardens it becomes basalt

orbit: a regular, repeating path that one object in space takes around another one

LEARN MORE

Adelman, Beth. *Birth of the Moon.* Minneapolis: Lerner Publications, 2025.

Britannica Kids: Moon
https://kids.britannica.com/students/article/Moon/275930

Hirsch, Rebecca E. *Mysteries of the Moon.* Minneapolis: Lerner Publications, 2021.

Huddleston, Emma. *Explore the Moon.* Minneapolis: Kids Core, an imprint of ABDO Publishing, 2022.

Lunar and Planetary Institute: Explore Marvel Moon
https://www.lpi.usra.edu/education/explore/marvelMoon

NASA Space Place: Moon
https://spaceplace.nasa.gov/search/moon

Rajczak, Michael. *Reaching the Moon.* New York: Gareth Stevens Publishing, 2021.

The Planetary Society: The Moon, Preserving Earth's Origin Story
https://www.planetary.org/worlds/the-moon

INDEX

PHOTO ACKNOWLEDGMENTS

Interior; Helen Field/Shutterstock, Interior; TB3XNW/Alamy, Interior; titoOnz/Alamy, p. 4; Galileo Galilei/Public domain/Wikimedia Commons, p. 5; NASA, p. 6; NASA, p. 7; NASA, p. 8; NASA, p.9, NASA/USSR, p. 10; John F. Kennedy Presidential Library and Museum, p. 11; NASA/Alexander Chernov, p. 12; NASA, p. 13; NASA, p. 14; NASA, p. 15; NASA, p. 16; NASA; p. 17; NASA/ISAS, p. 18; Jacques Dayan/Shutterstock, p. 19; NASA, p. 20; NASA, p. 21; ISRO/NASA/JPL-Caltech/Brown Univ./USGS, p. 22; NASA/ Arizona State University / Malin Space Science Systems, p. 23; NASA/Julia Bergeron, p. 24; NASA, p. 25; NASA, p. 26; NASA/Kim Shiflett, p. 27; NASA, p. 28; NASA, p. 29; joshimerbin/Shutterstock.

Cover: Digital Images Studio/ Shutterstock